101 Quotable Quotes and more on LEADERSHIP

Edited by
David Woods

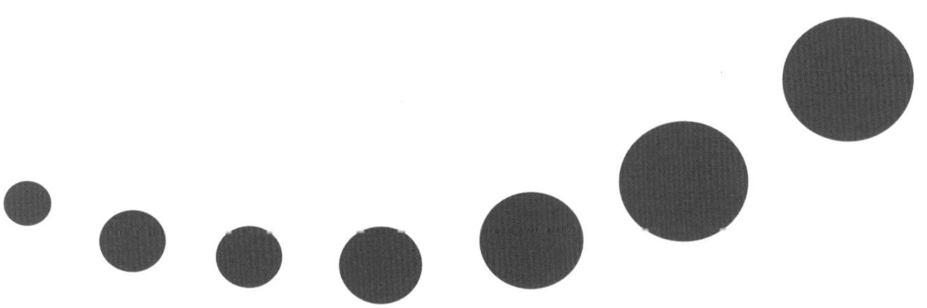

About the Editor

David Woods was the lead Education Adviser for London Schools and the London Challenge and then the Chief Adviser until April 2011, as well as being the Principal National Challenge Adviser for England. He was previously Head of the Department for Education and Skills (DfES) Advisory Service and before that the Chief Education Adviser for Birmingham Schools. He has spoken and written extensively about school improvement as well as leadership, teaching and learning.

David is currently the Chair of The London Leadership Strategy and several Local Authority Education Challenge Boards, as well as being a visiting Professor of Education at Warwick University and Institute of Education, University College, London.

Professor David Woods CBE

What is a quotation and why do we quote?

'It is a saying or piece of writing that strikes people as so true that they quote it or allude to it in speech or writing.'

Preface to the Oxford Dictionary of Modern Quotations

'By necessity, by proactivity – and by delight, we all quote!'

Ralph Waldo Emerson

'The Wisdom of the wise and the experience of ages, may be preserved by quotation.'

Benjamin Disraeli

'The power of quotation is as dreadful a weapon as any which the human intellect can forge.'

John Jay Chapman

'Engaging with the multiple potentials of quoting is how we live our lives, how we variously connect with others and with ourselves, with our past and our present.'

Ruth Finnegan

'Leadership is always important.
At great social turning points it is more important than ever. At times like these, the leadership we need is not leadership that turns us against others or holds us back in awe. It is leadership that lifts us up and turns us around together in pursuit of a common cause that expresses and advances our humanity.

Our schools are the social embryos of humanity - those institutions that are established to promote our highest collective values. They should be the embodiment of norms of reciprocity, active trust, and democratic deliberation. It is not more mandates and management they need, but the broad shoulders of uplifting and sustainable leadership'.

Andy Hargreaves and Dennis Shirley

The Fourth Way

Introduction

This is primarily a book on quotations for school and educational leadership, although some quotations have been taken from successful leaders of other organisations and leadership thinkers and commentators generally.

Everyone agrees that leadership matters greatly in all fields of endeavour and that is why there is so much attention paid to it today. In the past 20 years there has been a huge growth in published literature about educational leadership in particular with articles, specialist journals and books and it is a rich area of ongoing research.

In the literature on leadership some of the leadership theories centre on the personal disposition of the leader, their personality and character. Others refer to the behaviour of leaders, identifying different styles and roles and yet others concentrate on leadership in specific contexts.

In education generally leadership is increasingly viewed as the quality of the relationship between leaders and followers and most of the debate has concentrated upon two contrasting leadership styles: transactional and transformational.

In transactional leadership the relationship between leaders and followers is based on an exchange of value that is mutually beneficial, meeting demands both ways. In such an approach the emphasis will tend to be on the management of school systems and structures.

Transformational leadership does more than explore and meet existing needs or demands from followers. It focuses on the people involved and relationships and seeks to transform attitudes and beliefs. Transformational leaders try to unleash the motivation that drives followers and meet that higher need, seeking to develop a mature, stimulating relationship that will secure the maximum 'discretionary effort'.

Transformational leadership is an idea that has been steadily gaining ground and the idea of a leader who is inspirational and visionary and able to engage the emotions of individuals and communities has obvious appeal. However, most educational leaders will recognise that these are not entirely opposite styles characterised crudely as 'preoccupied with purpose, values, morals and ethics' or preoccupied by 'power, position, politics and perks'.

In reality school leaders need to establish particular elements of transactional management systems to support the best leadership and managerial leadership is a vital part of the armoury of any successful headteacher. Schools that are overled and undermanaged are just as ineffective as schools who are underled and overmanaged. The best leaders know that it is crucially important to 'do the right things and do things right', aligning internal structures and systems to overarching values and goals.

Although much of modern leadership theory focuses on the personal qualities of the leader there is widespread discontent with the motion of 'heroic' or 'charismatic' leadership when applied to educational leadership, mainly because such leaders are role models who can never be emulated and often encourage dependency on others. Currently there is an emphasis on 'authentic leadership', which maintains that the best leaders make the most of the qualities they already possess, trading on their strengths and understanding their weaknesses. Authentic leadership requires heightened self-awareness with an emphasis on vision, values, integrity and beliefs. Leaders are expected to ground their actions in clear personal and professional values that represent their moral purpose and help them develop a specific vision for the school.

Increasingly, writers on leadership have recognised the importance of followership in the leadership equation with a transference of experience and emotions as a powerful motivating factor. There is a recognition that we can expect far too much from 'the leader' given the complexities of modern schooling and hence the present leadership emphasis upon 'invitational' and 'distributed leadership' – from individuals to groups and teams where 'distributed leadership' is crucial to the development of a sustained capacity for school improvement.

There is an understanding that the first rule of leadership is that it is shared and that school leaders exist throughout the organisation from student leaders to senior leaders. Distributed leadership concentrates on engaging expertise wherever it exists rather than seeking this only through formal position or role. Research indicates that distributed leadership expands the scope of leadership leading to increased student outcomes whilst developing the formal leaders of the future. There is a growing literature in particular on the vital importance of middle leaders – the so-called 'engine room' of the school. Middle leaders have a great opportunity to make a difference for pupils not only through their direct impact as teachers but also getting the best out of everyone in their teams.

Beyond even invitational or distributed leadership there is the concept of 'elective' leadership where students and staff put forward ideas to lead particular projects and programmes, although of course there needs to be the right leadership culture and climate to encourage this. There is an increasing realisation that students can be active leaders in their schools, participating in the construction of their own learning environments and anything else that happens in and around schools.

The increasing focus on teaching and learning as the core business of schools has led to an emphasis upon 'instructional leadership', which is primarily concerned with the behaviour of teachers and teaching assistants as they engage in activities directly affecting the success of their students. In the past few years the term 'instructional leadership' has been broadened to the notion of 'learning-centred leadership', which has greater potential to impact both on school and student outcomes with a central focus on the 'learning school'.

Context, of course, will always be important in school leadership. For example, there has been particular research on models of school leadership in challenging urban environments or leading schools out of 'special measures', that emphasises particular qualities, behaviours and responses.

Some school leaders succeed brilliantly as 'turn around' leaders in challenging schools but many struggle in a second headship in a relatively easier school. Equally there are some well qualified 'instructional' leaders who can't bring about necessary improvements in underperforming schools because they struggle to motivate staff and students.

Whatever the context, leaders will need to lead through example, setting appropriate expectations with encouragement and enthusiasm to generate energy, willing effort and above all empowerment, trusting people and giving them the opportunity to do their best. In these endeavours the proper use of language is vital. Careless and negative talk can sap energy and demotivate, whilst positive and targeted talk can spark enthusiasm, extra effort and increase aspirational thinking.

Whatever the leadership styles or behaviours, the success of a school is going to be judged by impact and outcomes reported every year in the form of performance indicators and periodically through inspection reports. Leaders are highly accountable to the extent that they even lose their jobs and this can affect the way they practise leadership. Because of this it is important to define 'success'. In our book, *What Makes a Good School Now?*, Tim Brighouse and I have written that we would want schools to be places where:

- The full range of success – academic, sporting, artistic, practical support for others, triumph over adversity – is celebrated.

- All pupils are increasingly aware of their progress and potential and that this is without limit if they make the effort.

- Everyone is anxious to improve on their own and shared achievement.

- Everyone feels fulfilled in what they do and contributes to the fulfilment of others.

- All members of the school community are committed to their own continuous learning and support that of others.

- Everyone is aware of the school's collective past and present success and is ambitious to contribute to that collective legacy for the future.

Such a school could not succeed without determined and extended leadership widely practised throughout the school.

A considerable amount of research has been conducted nationally and internationally into effective school leadership, stimulated in our country by the establishment of the first National College for Leadership in the world in 2002. In 2006 the National College published an overview of findings from research evidence *(Seven Strong Claims about Effective School Leadership, Leithwood et al).*

The seven claims are as follows:-

- School leadership is second only to classroom teaching as an influence on pupil learning;
- Almost all successful leaders draw on the same basic repertoire of leadership practices (the main elements are: building vision, developing people, redesigning the organisation, managing teaching and learning);
- The ways in which leaders apply these basic leadership practices, not the practices themselves, demonstrate responsiveness to the contexts in which they work;
- School leaders improve teaching and learning indirectly through their influence on staff motivation, commitment and working conditions;
- School leadership has a greater influence on schools and students when it is widely distributed;
- Some patterns of distribution are more effective than others; and
- A small handful of personal traits explain a high proportion of the variation in leadership effectiveness.

Their main conclusion "that there is not a single documented case of a school successfully turning around its pupil achievement trajectory in the absence of talented leadership," endorses the vital role of school leaders at all levels and in all contexts. In 2007 the Department for Education commissioned an independent study into school leadership from PriceWaterhouseCoopers, which concluded that many of the challenges faced by school leaders are driven by the increase in the scale and complexity of agendas that school leaders have to take forward. They recommended diversifying leadership models, facilitating greater distributed leadership with accountability, building leadership capacity programmes, and greater attention to talent management and succession planning.

Since then there have been several seminal publications related to the essential tasks and requirements for leaders, including Rob Goffee and Gareth Jones' challenging title *Why should anybody be led by you?* and David Pendleton and Adrian Furnham's rather grand claim *Leadership – All you need to know.* These books relate to research in leadership in different fields but they have been applied to school and educational leadership in particular. The latter's five requirements for leaders are an example. Leaders should:

- **Inspire** – create excitement, idealism and confidence about what is possible.

- **Focus** – prioritise and sequence – plan in detail, make the steps clear and do what is required.

- **Enable** – give people scope to act and ensure they do what is required of them.

- **Reinforce** – the creation of appropriate consequences – celebrate success and deal with underperformance.

- **Learn** – learning and reflection are at the core of continuous improvement.

Tim Brighouse and I have also produced a list of six essential tasks for school leaders (*The A-Z of School Improvement*):

- Create, energy, enthusiasm, commitment and hope.
- Build capacity through developing staff and students.
- Meet and minimise crisis.
- Secure and enhance the learning environment.
- Seek and chart improvement.
- Extend the vision of what's possible.

Other recent literature such as Fenton Whelan on *Lessons Learned*, Daniel Goleman's book on *Focus: The Hidden Driver of Excellence* and several books by Michael Fullan including *The Principal*, have added to the debate. Fenton Whelan has stressed the importance of creating the right programmes to apprentice and develop school leaders, selecting the right people for leadership positions, empowering and encouraging leaders and intervening quickly to tackle ineffective school leadership.

Daniel Goleman, who had previously written about leadership styles and the importance of building and sustaining relationships, has now stressed in his book on 'Focus', the key importance of leaders directing attention to where it needs to go. He describes this as "the primal task of leadership with the best leaders able to shift attention to the right place at the right time, sensing trends and emerging realities and seizing opportunities." Michael Fullan talks in his latest book, *The Principal*, about three keys to maximising impact - leading learning, being a system player and being a change agent.

From the literature associated with the London Challenge and the London Leadership Strategy and writers such as Michael Fullan, David Hargreaves and Robert Hill, there has been a focus on 'system leadership' with the best school leaders encouraged to take responsibility not just for leading their own schools but supporting other schools across the system.

National Leaders of Education (NLEs) were first established in 2006 with the primary purpose of raising standards by harnessing the skills and experiences of the best school leaders to support those that needed to improve. National Teaching Schools were also established in 2010 with a remit to focus on the quality of teaching and leadership, providing high quality training and development. With them came the creation of Specialist Leaders of Education (SLEs), excellent professionals in leadership positions below the headteacher who support other individuals or teams in similar positions in other schools.

Since the White Paper of 2010 there has been a considerable expansion of NLEs, Teaching Schools and SLEs as a means of driving a system of school-led improvement. These developments have demanded an extra set of skills than institutional leadership, such as providing expert diagnosis and improvement planning for another school, supporting and challenging external senior leaders through focused conversations, coaching and mentoring and devising bespoke solutions in another context. In this sense the best school leaders have become system players and change agents beyond their own borders.

Very recently (May, 2015), the Department for Education has published new National Standards of Excellence for headteachers, replacing the 2004 National Standards. The Standards are set out in four domains - qualities and knowledge, pupils and staff, systems and process and the self-improving system. With each domain there are key characteristics expected of headteachers and by implication, of all school leaders. In the domain of qualities and knowledge, headteachers are expected to:

- Hold and articulate clear values and moral purpose, focused on providing a world-class education for the pupils they serve.

- Demonstrate optimistic personal behaviour, positive relationships and attitudes towards their pupils and staff, and toward parents, governors and members of the local community.

- Lead by example - with integrity, creativity, resilience and clarity - drawing on their own scholarship, expertise and skills, and that of those around them.

- Sustain wide, current knowledge and understanding of education and school systems locally, nationally and globally and pursue continuous professional development.

- Work with political and financial astuteness, within a clear set of principles centred on the school's vision, ably translating local and national policy into the school's context.

- Communicate compellingly the school's vision and drive the strategic leadership, empowering all pupils and staff to excel.

Whatever the type and range of school leadership there seems to be an emerging consensus in the literature that in 21st Century leadership the key aspects are vision, creating alignment and motivation; building commitment and empowering others in pursuit of the best possible outcomes. The London Leadership Strategy has published the *9 Pillars of Greatness* based on research into the literature and the experiences of outstanding school leaders. One of the pillars is entitled 'Inspirational leadership at all levels throughout the school' with a list of features and characteristics, which are set out on pages 26 and 27. It maintains that in schools with the best leadership there would be a widely observed sense of aspiration, ambition and moral purpose; clarity and critical analysis; creativity, trust and transparency; courage and consistency together with hope and humility. The quotations that follow exemplify all of these characteristics and more and will hopefully inspire all school leaders in their endeavours to create and sustain excellent schools.

David Woods
May, 2015

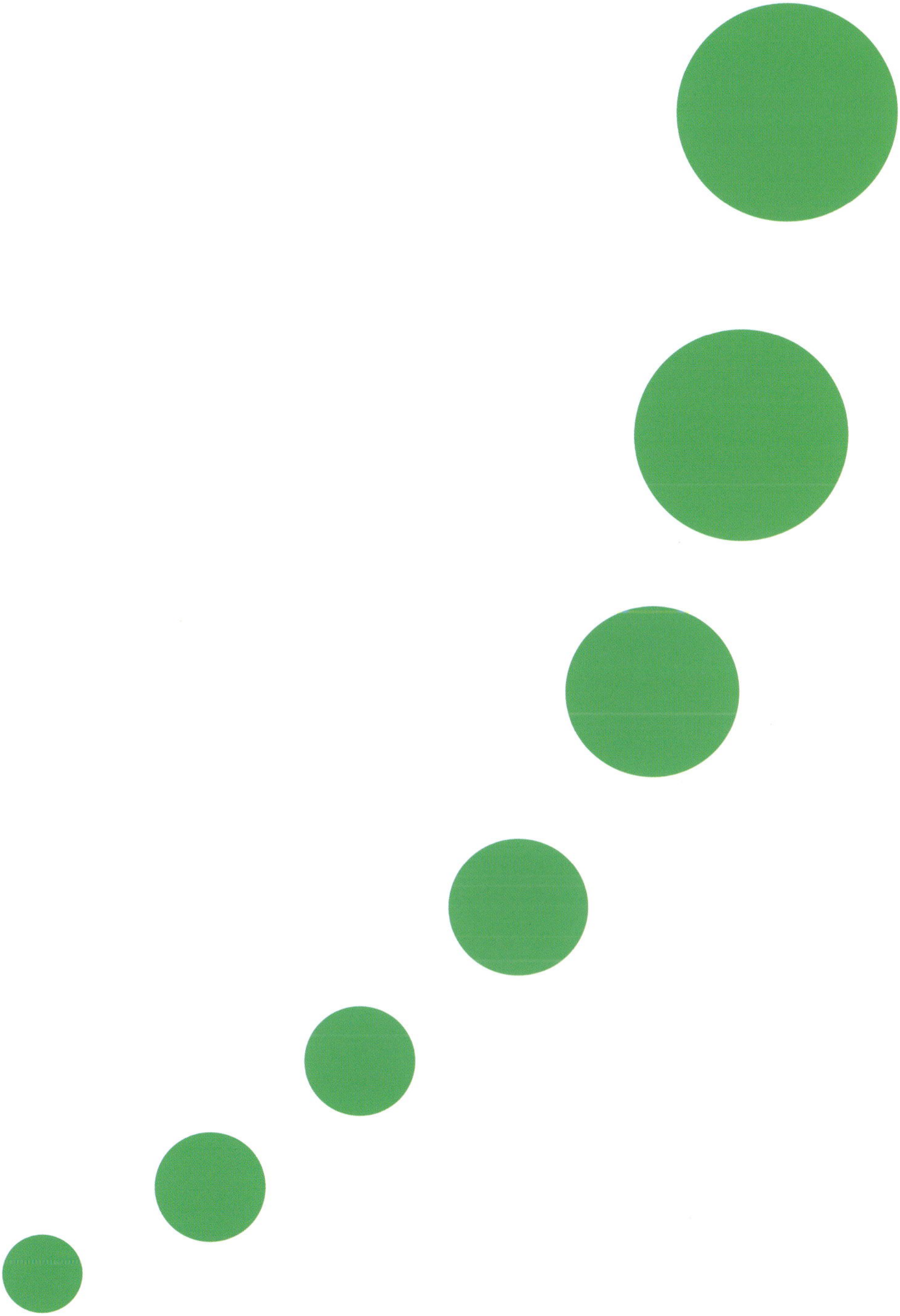

Definitions of leadership

'A definition of leadership is to create the conditions for people to thrive, individually and collectively, and achieve significant goals'.

David Pendleton and Adrian Furnham
Leadership: All you Need to Know

'Leadership is lifting a person's vision to high sights, the raising of a person's performance to a higher standard, the building of a personality beyond its normal limitations'.

Peter Drucker
Managing in a Time of Great Change

‘Leadership can be defined as the will to control events, the understanding to chart a course, and the power to get a job done co-operatively using the skills and abilities of other people’.

Donald Krause

‘A leader is an individual who significantly affects the thoughts, feelings and behaviours of a significant number of individuals’.

Howard Gardner
Leading Minds: An Anatomy of Leadership

Inspirational leadership at all levels throughout the school

- The school's leadership is transformational - visionary, inspiring and values-based. Leaders are able to envision and share a compelling view of the school in the future; they communicate this effectively to the entire school community. Leaders are cheerleaders, enthusiasts, forecasters and dramatists.

- There is excellent operational leadership. Leaders are planners, organisers, resourcers, tacticians and deliverers. They pay attention to detail and get results; they are resilient and determined.

- The school's leadership is transactional – based on building and sustaining high quality relationships between leaders and the led. Leaders are nurturers, trainers, mentors and coaches.

- The school practises invitational and distributed leadership (between staff and students), based on the belief that all have potential for growth and development, in the knowledge that everyone has a different profile of leadership qualities and with an understanding that the best leaders in one situation may not be the most effective in another. Shared leadership demonstrates mutual respect and trust.

- Leaders deliberately build on the capacity for growth and adaptation to change through careful recruitment and retention, developing the workforce and fostering learning in the workplace. They see innovation as part of their day-to-day activity.

- Leaders strive to create and embed aspiration and ambition and develop creativity, wider learning and supported risk taking.

- Leaders develop an optimistic, lively, energising environment to maximise the additional effort of members of the school community.

- Extended and system-wide leadership are widely practised through school-to-school collaboration, the building of networks and quality relationships with outside agencies, and the provision of an infrastructure for new approaches and change.

- Leadership characteristics widely observed in the school include a sense of moral purpose, clarity, creativity, transparency, resilience, energy, enthusiasm, hope and humility.

The Nine Pillars of Greatness
London Leadership Strategy

Quotes on Leadership

'The art of the headteacher, as skald or story teller, encompasses imagery, metaphor, simile, analogy, and an unerring sense of time and occasion'.

Tim Brighouse
How Successful Headteachers Survive and Thrive

'Efficiency is doing things right. Effectiveness is doing the right things'.

Peter Drucker
Managing in a Time of Great Change

'Distributed leadership draws change <u>from</u> the everyday knowledge and capacities of staff rather than doing reforms <u>through</u>. It is a crucial element in sustainable leadership. Distributed leadership is grounded in and advances a compelling moral purpose'.

Andy Hargreaves and Dennis Shirley
The Fourth Way

‘Headteachers are the gatekeepers and gate-openers of their schools. Connecting with what is ‘out there’ in ways that really matter for pupils is almost impossible without their leadership, intervention and support’.

Andy Hargreaves and Michael Fullan
What’s Worth Fighting for in Education?

‘Leadership is all about turning fear into confidence, creating clarity from confusion and mobilising people in pursuit of a better future’.

Matt Church
The Success Zone

‘This is the common factor about leading successful schools – teachers grow in a collaborative culture through the establishment of feedback for growth and transparency about practice and results. Healthy pressure (high expectations) and support (both technical and emotional) helps peers to grow’.

Michael Fullan
The Principal: Three Keys to Maximising Impact

'As a middle leader in a school you probably have the potential to make more difference to the outcomes for pupils than any other group of staff. It is an often quoted cliché, but middle leaders really are the engine room of the school. It is your team that delivers at the front line: great teaching, strong support and guidance, and excellent curriculum, all delivered in a great climate for learning. These all add up to great outcomes for pupils'.

Andy Buck, Oli Tomlinson and James Toop
What Makes a Great Middle Leader?

'Good leadership is reliably, rigorously, robustly and relentlessly doing the right things with the right people at the right time'.

David Woods

'Rather than hoping for a godlike, heroic leader, who will see the way forward and through their skilful, entrepreneurial strategies pull our institution forward, the institutions that thrive will find ways to foster leadership at all levels'.

James Krantz

‘Great leadership matters - from the front line of the school to the Headteacher it is the most important advantage any school can have’.

Rod Eddington

‘Directing attention to where it needs to go is a primal task of leadership. Talent here lies in the ability to shift attention to the right place at the right time, sensing trends and emerging realities and seizing opportunities’.

Daniel Goleman
Focus: The Hidden Driver of Excellence

‘The more leaders focus their relationships, their work and their own learning on the core business of teaching and learning, the greater their influence on student outcomes’.

Viviane Robinson
Student-Centred Leadership

'The five 'e' factors of leadership for motivation are example, enthusiasm, expectations, encouragement and empowerment'.

David Woods

'The skill for the successful leader is to get the right balance between personal accountability and the accountability of others. Ultimately what the leader does sets the tone. Good leaders will take responsibility for results, are clear on how they are going to communicate, how well they are doing, and how others are doing'.

Andy Buck
What Makes a Great School?

'Leadership is about congruence – not heroic, not distributed, but congruent with the values of the organisation and the task in hand'.

Ruth Silver

'Ensuring that every school has excellent leadership means four things: creating the right programmes to apprentice and develop school leaders, selecting the right people for leadership positions, empowering and encouraging leaders and intervening quickly to tackle ineffective school leadership'.

Fenton Whelan

Lessons Learned

‘High performers work together and in so doing gain our admiration and respect. They do things we can mimic but never reproduce so the best we can hope for is to learn from them and create our own act’.

Alistair Smith
High Performers, The Secrets of Successful Schools

‘You can mandate awful to good but you cannot mandate greatness – that has to be unleashed’.

Joel Klein

‘Perhaps the key task of any institution is to encourage a growth mindset. When that kind of philosophy becomes embedded in a culture, the consequences can be dramatic’.

Matthew Syed
Bounce: The Myth of Talent and the Power of Practice

‘Great leaders know how to get the right people on the bus, the wrong people off the bus, and the right people in the right seats’.

Jim Collins
Good to Great

‘The intelligent school understands that it is important to share or distribute responsibility throughout the school avoiding a culture of top down change and instead creating a culture in which teachers are given real leadership roles and responsibilities...’.

Barbara MacGilchrist, Kate Myers and Jane Reed
The Intelligent School

‘Charismatic leaders inadvertently often do more harm than good because, at best, they provide episodic involvement followed by frustrated or despondent dependency. Superhuman leaders also do us another disservice: they are role models who can never be emulated by large numbers. Deep and sustained reform depends on many of us, not just on the very few who are destined to be extraordinary’.

Michael Fullan
The Principal

'The principals of tomorrow's schools must be instructional leaders who possess the requisite skills, capacities and commitment to lead the accountability parade, not follow it. Excellence in school leadership should be recognised as the most important component of school reform. Without leadership, the chances for systemic improvement in teaching and learning are nil'.

Gerald Tirazzi

'Where there is no vision, the people perish'.

Proverbs, The Bible

'At the heart of successful leadership is a more than passing competence in three processes or skills, namely delegation, time management and the management of change'.

Tim Brighouse and David Woods
How to Improve Your School

'Creative leadership is an imaginative and thought-through response to opportunities and to challenging issues that inhibit learning at all levels. It is about seeing, thinking and doing things differently to improve the life chances of all students'.

Louise Stoll

'Work settings are language communities....All leaders are leading language communities. Though every person, in every setting, has some opportunity to influence the nature of the language, leaders have exponentially greater access and opportunity to shape, alter or ratify the existing language rules'.

Kegan and Lahey

How the Way We Talk Can Change the Way We Work

'The foundations of successful urban leadership are a robust sense of purpose, driven by courage and conviction and enduring personal resilience characterised by a sense of optimism that change can and will happen'.

A Model of School Leadership in Challenging Urban Environments

'Discretionary effort is the effort that does not have to be given, but it is given because the individual chooses to do so...it is through (leaders) creating engagement and team working that the commitment builds and discretionary effort increases'.

David Pendleton and Adrian Furnham
Leadership: All you Need to Know

'A school without a vision is a vacuum inviting intrusion'.

Roland S. Barth
Improving Schools

'Excellent school leaders create schools in which teachers and students who might struggle elsewhere can perform to a high standard. They set high expectations, create an environment in which students and teachers are supported to achieve them, and carefully manage teaching, learning and improvement'.

Fenton Whelan
Lessons Learned

'For leaders to get results they need three kinds of focus. Inner focus attunes our intuitions, guiding values, and better decisions. Other focus smooths our connections to the people in our lives. Outer focus lets us navigate in the larger world. A leader turned out of his internal world will be rudderless; one blind to the world of others will be clueless; those indifferent to the larger systems within which they operate will be blindsided... Leaders need the full range of inner, other and outer focus to excel - a weakness in any one of them can throw a leader off balance.'

Daniel Goleman

Focus: The Hidden Driver of Excellence

'Once a commitment is made, the goal will seem larger, bolder, and more exciting... Leaders need to fix on it like a laser beam. They need to see intensely, even obsessively. They feel it. They hear it. They taste it. They smell it. It becomes part of them, their very identity, because it is something they are committed to make happen, come what may, whatever it takes.'

Stephen Denning

The Secret Language of Leadership

'We tend to overstate how outgoing leaders need to be – most leading is done through small meetings and at a distance'.

Susan Cain
Quiet

'Vision is the ability to see what is unseen, realise what has yet to be, and act upon one's beliefs in the face of uncertainty'.

Jerome Freiberg

'The focus for leadership in actively improving schools is the creation and expansion of improvement capacity – a complex blend of structural and cultural development combined with an evolving contextual and theoretical knowledge base. Such capacity change – culture, structure, knowledge – supports continuous organisational and professional renewal'.

David Hopkins
School Improvement for Real

'The inner belief and commitment to leading excellence by those who lead schools is the starting point. At its beating heart the excellent school is in a place where people care more than others think is wise, work more than others think is safe, dream more than others think is practical, and expect more than others think is possible'.

Roy Blatchford
The Restless School

'Leadership is not domination, but the art of persuading people to work towards a common goal'.

Daniel Goleman
The New Leader

'Leaders do the right thing when they focus, not on their own needs and wants, but on the people affected by their action'.

Robert Sutton

'Your first and foremost job as a leader is to manage your own energy and how to manage the energy of those around you'.

Steve Radcliffe

'System leadership is not leading just one or more schools, not even many schools, but leading the education system as a whole and doing so with an explicit moral purpose in mind, with the implications for actions'.

David Hargreaves

'The old model of transactional leadership is based on the idea that if you do this, then we'll do this. It is a very simple equation. Transformational leadership is much more inspirational. It is about engaging the emotions of individuals in the organisation. It is crucial for leading change today'.

Alan Hooper

'A turnaround leader must facilitate a psychological turnaround of attitudes and behaviour before organisational recovery can take place'.

Rosabeth Moss Kanter
Harvard Business Review

'For schools to be successful staff have to be constantly pushed to develop their teaching and learning. The school leader needs to take charge of that – providing the tools, the support and the direction to make staff development part of the fabric of the institution'.

Tim Brighouse and David Woods
What Makes a Good School Now?

'The very essence of leadership is that you have a vision. It's got to be a vision that you articulate clearly and forcefully on every occasion. You can't blow an uncertain trumpet'.

Theodore Hesburgh

'It is these middle leaders, who have a microscopic focus on every teacher in their department, who are going to really shift things – a headteacher can't line manage everyone'.

James Toop

'I take my stand on detail.'

Edward Thring
Victorian Headmaster

'Good leadership, courageous leadership, opens horizons and extends the vision of what is possible and then knows how to take steps to turn the vision into reality'.

Steve Munby

'Outstanding leaders think and act systematically. In contrast to good leaders, the outstanding leaders see wholes, move fluidly from element to element and join up their thinking and the organisation's activity. Central to all this is a keen sense of purpose and their understanding of how different aspects of organisations internally connect. Purpose drives performance and the outstanding leaders both understand this and refuse to allow anything to stand in the way'.

John Pendleton and Adrian Furnham

Leadership: All you Need to Know

‘A good leader takes more than their fair share of the blame and gives more than their share of the credit’.

Arnold Colesnow

‘We must believe that we are gifted for something, and that this thing, at whatever cost, must be attained’.

Marie Curie

‘The behaviours of school leaders have a greater influence on pupil performance than school structures or models’.

PriceWaterhouseCoopers
Independent Report into School Leadership

'There is a wealth of evidence that the quality of leaders positively enhances teaching and learning'.

Alma Harris
Distributed School Leadership

'You can't direct the wind but you can adjust the sails'.

Anon

'If you want to be a leader, you have to be a real human being. You must recognise the true meaning of life before you can become a great leader. You must understand yourself first'.

Peter Senge
The Fifth Discipline: The Art and Practice of the Learning Organisation

'If your actions inspire others to dream more, learn more, do more and become more, then you are a leader'.

John Quincy Adams

'Optimism is the faith that leads to achievement; nothing can be done without hope and confidence'.

Helen Keller

'The role of the principal needs to be balanced between content and organisational leadership. These competencies involve building instructional leadership into the culture of the school and building strong leadership in teachers. The educational leader is the overall leader of instruction, but he or she needs to have time and skills to motivate and build teams and develop leadership capacity for change'.

Lyle Kirtman
Leadership and Teams: The Missing Piece of the Education Reform Puzzle

‘It is especially important to be forward looking in the context of education. The crucial words to keep in mind are those which point ahead: hope, intention, expectation’.

Bodil Jonsson
Ten Thoughts about Time

‘The real voyage of discovery consists, not in seeking new landscapes, but in having new eyes’.

Marcel Proust

‘Outstanding leaders have a vision for their schools – a mental picture of a preferred future – which is shared with all in the school community and which shapes the programme for learning and teaching as well as policies, priorities, plans and procedures pervading the day-to-day life of the school’.

Hedley Beare, Brian J. Caldwell and Ross H. Millikan
Creating an Excellent School

'Today's effective principal constructs a shared vision with members of the school community, convenes the conversations, insists on a student learning focus, evokes and supports leadership in others, models and participates in collaborative practices, helps pose the questions, and facilitates dialogue that addresses the confounding issues of practice. This work requires skill and new understanding; it is much easier to tell or manage than it is to perform as a collaborative instructional leader'.

Linda Lambert

'Nothing great was every achieved without enthusiasm'.

Ralph Waldo Emerson

'It is unlikely that you will be able to inspire, excite and motivate others unless you can show who you are and what you stand for'.

Robert Goffee and Gareth Jones
Why Should Anybody be Led by You?

'Trust underpins and affects the quality of any relationship, every connection, every work project...it changes the quality of every present moment and alters the trajectory and outcomes of every future'.

Stephen Covey
The Speed of Trust

'The important thing is not to stop questioning'.

Albert Einstein

'One of the defining characteristics of highly effective leadership teams is that they have a common language based on a shared vocabulary, agreed definitions and mutual understanding. The best way to achieve this is through regular, structured dialogue.'

John West-Burnham and David Harris
Leadership Dialogues

'Language can make or break a school. Careless talk can sap energy or offend; targeted talk can motivate and increase aspirational thinking; positive talk can spark enthusiasm and a willingness to go the extra mile; and negative talk can demotivate and create an unpleasant environment. Leaders need to consider carefully the language used'.

Tim Brighouse and David Woods
The A-Z of School Improvement

'You cannot achieve a new goal by applying the same level of thinking that got you where you are today'.

Albert Einstein

'Almost all successful leaders draw on the same repertoire of leadership practices; the main elements being building vision, developing people, re-designing the organisation and managing teaching and learning'

Keith Leithwood et al
Seven Strong Claims About Effective School Leadership

'Successful leaders are relentlessly curious about their key people – the motives, values, skills and passions of their people are essential parts of the context'.

Robert Goffee and Gareth Jones
Why Should Anybody be Led by You?

'Leadership is action not position'.

Donald H. McGannon

'Headship involves being both a historian and futurologist. Any leader wishing to extend the vision of what's possible is deeply aware of this double requirement: the present dominates so much of school life. Telling stories which remind people of past success is a wise thing to do alongside being forecasters of the weather and describers of future possibilities'.

Tim Brighouse
How Successful Headteachers Survive and Thrive

'People are most motivated, energised and self-efficacious when they feel that they have overcome obstacles and made progress. School leaders should create the conditions that help people succeed. This means removing obstacles, providing resources and supporting group development and the calling of attention to progress made through celebration...this is in keeping with the natural design of the human spirit, to do something intrinsically worthwhile with others in a collective effort.'

Teresa Amabile and Steven Kramer

The Progress Principle

'Perpetual optimism is a force multiplier. The ripple effect of a leader's enthusiasm is awesome. So is the impact of cynicism and pessimism. Spare me the grim litany of the 'realist', give me the unrealistic aspirations of the optimist any day'.

General Colin Powell

'Never doubt that a small group of thoughtful, committed people can change the world. Indeed, it is the only thing that ever has'.

Margaret Mead

'Remember that some people make things happen, some people watch things happen and some people wonder what happened'.

Anon

'The great gift of leadership is to bring about the gifts of fellowship in everybody else'.

Michael Fullan
The Moral Imperative of School Leadership

'Leaders cannot be taught – but leaders can be educated'.

Anon

'There is a difference between leadership and management. Leadership is of the spirit, compounded of personality and vision; its practice is an art. Management is of the mind, a matter of accurate calculation…its practice is a science. Managers are necessary; leaders are essential'.

Field Marshal Lord Slim
Quoted in Van Maurik, Writers on Leadership

'For leadership to be everywhere, it must be embedded deeply both throughout the school and in the school community. In successful schools leadership density rules'.

T.J. Sergiovanni
Leadership: What's in it for Schools?

'The first rule of leadership is that it is shared'.

Tim Brighouse and David Woods
How to Improve Your School

'Leadership is to the current decade what standards were to the 1990s for those interested in large-scale reform. Standards, even when well implemented, can take us only part way to large-scale reform. It is only leadership that can take us all the way'.

Michael Fullan
Change Forces with a Vengeance

'Leaders set the course for the organisation; managers make sure the course is followed. Leaders make strategic plans; managers design operational systems for carrying out the plans. Leaders stimulate and inspire; managers use their interpersonal influence and authority to translate that energy into productive work'.

K.S. Louis and M.B. Miles
Improving the Urban High School

'Planning is bringing the future into the present so that you can do something about it now'.

Alan Lakein

'Leadership, like jazz, is a public performance, dependent on so many things – the environment, the volunteers in the band, the need for everybody to perform as individuals and as a group, the absolute dependence of the leader on the members of the band'.

Max De Pree
Leadership Jazz

'Setting an example is not the main means of influencing people; it is the only means'.

Albert Einstein

'Good leaders are adept at reframing problems, at putting old facts into new bottles, or reconceptualising the familiar so that new solutions leap up'.

Charles B. Handy
Inside Organisations

'School leadership is a profoundly moral, ethical and emotional activity designed to encourage a school's staff to build and act on a shared and evolving vision of enhanced educational experiences for pupils'.

Louise Stoll and Dean Fink
It's About Learning and it's About Time

'Make no mistake: Leadership is about results. Great leadership has the potential to excite people to extraordinary levels of achievement....Leaders at all levels make a difference to performance'.

Jim Collins
Good to Great

'Better is possible. It does not take genius. It takes diligence, it takes moral clarity. It takes ingenuity. And above all, it takes a willingness to try'.

Atul Gawande
Better

'As for the best leaders, the one factor that differentiates them from the rest is not skill or qualifications but mindset.... they have exceptionally high aspirations, courage to take people further than they thought possible and huge resilience in the face of adversity'.

Jo Owen
The Mindset of Success

'Leadership for transformation is the art of accomplishing more than the science of management says is possible'.

General Colin Powell

'A good leader is also a good follower'.

American proverb

'One of the key principles of leadership is that leaders must strive to be model learners. They must continue to read, and engage in discussions about all manner of subjects as well as the most recent theories of learning. As leaders they should question current practices, and never feel that they have progressed beyond the point of being a learner. Learning is truly a lifelong experience and cannot be thought of simply as a destination'.

T.J. Sergiovanni
Leadership: What's in it for Schools?

Level Five Leaders:

- Are ambitious for their organisation, not for themselves
- Talk about their organisation, not about themselves
- Have a dogged, unwavering, ferocious resolve
- Are fanatically driven with an incurable need to produce substantial results
- Are more like plough horses than show horses
- Apportion credit to events outside themselves when things go well
- Take personal responsibility when things go badly
- Set up their successors for even greater success.

Level five leaders blend extreme personal humility with intense professional will'.

Jim Collins

Good to Great

'Teachers who choose the path of teacher leadership become owners and investors in their schools, rather than mere tenants'.

Roland S. Barth
Improving Schools From Within

'The task of leadership is not to put greatness into humanity but to elicit it, for the greatness is already there'.

John Buchan
Montrose and Leadership

'School leaders should continue to remind staff of why and how past improvements were made. This ensures staff defining new actions have a contextual history to reflect upon and do not continually 'redesign the wheel'. They should also ensure that the school's learning journey is passed on to those who come after them'.

George Berwick
Moral Capital

'It is better to lead from behind and put others in front, especially when you celebrate the victory when nice things occur. You take the front line when there is danger. Then people will appreciate your leadership'.

Nelson Mandela

Quotes from Business and Politics

'The greatest glory in living lies not in never failing, but in rising every time we fail'.

Martin Luther King

'Whether you think you can, or you think you can't - you're right'.

Henry Ford

'Leadership and learnership are indispensable to one another'.

John F. Kennedy

'Courage is rightly esteemed the first of human qualities because as has been said, it is the quality which guarantees all others'.

Winston S. Churchill
Great Contemporaries

'You gain strength, courage and confidence by every experience in which you really stop to look fear in the face. You must do the thing you think you cannot do'.

Eleanor Roosevelt

'People who are unable to motivate themselves must be content with mediocrity, no matter how impressive their other talents'.

Andrew Carnegie

'Teamwork is the fuel that allows common people to achieve uncommon results.'

Andrew Carnegie

'You have to look at leadership through the eyes of the followers and you have to live the message. What I have learned is that people become motivated when you guide them to the source of their own power and when you make heroes out of employees who personify what you want to see in the organisation'.

Anita Roddick

'Be a yardstick of quality. Some people aren't used to an environment where excellence is expected'.

Steve Jobs

'Start with good people, lay out the rules, communicate with your employees, motivate them and reward them. If you do all these things effectively, you can't miss'.

Lee Iacocca

Talking Straight

'Before you are a leader, success is all about growing yourself. When you become a leader, success is all about growing others'.

Jack Welch

'True leadership lies in guiding others to success. In ensuring that everyone is performing at their best, doing the work they are pledged to do and doing it well'.

Bill Owens

'This is the true joy in in life, being used for a purpose recognised by yourself as a mighty one; the being a force of nature instead of a feverish, selfish little clod of ailments and grievances complaining that the world will not devote itself to making you happy. I am of the opinion that my life belongs to the whole community, and as long as I live it is my privilege to do for it whatever I can. I want to be thoroughly used up when I die, for the harder I work the more I live. I rejoice in life for its own sake. Life is no 'brief candle' to me. It is a sort of splendid torch which I have got hold of for the moment, and I want to make it burn as brightly as possible, before handing it on to future generations'.

George Bernard Shaw

Man and Superman

Sources and references

Amabile, T & Kramer, S (2011)
The Progress Principle
Harvard Business Review Press

Barber M, Whelan, F & Clark, M (2010)
Capturing the Leadership Premium: How The World's Top School Systems are Building Leadership Capacity for the Future
McKinsey & Co

Barth, R.S (1990)
Improving Schools from Within
Jossey-Bass

Beare, H, Caldwell, B.T & Millikan, R.H (1990)
Creating an Excellent School
Routledge

Blatchford, R (2014)
The Restless School
John Catt Education

Brighouse, T.M & Woods, D.C (1999)
How to Improve Your School
Routledge

Brighouse, T.M & Woods, D.C (2008)
What Makes a Good School Now?
Continuum

Brighouse, T.M & Woods, D.C (2013)
The A-Z of School Improvement.
Bloomsbury

Brighouse, T.M (2007)
How Successful Headteachers Survive and Thrive
RM Publications

Brighouse, T.M & Davies, B (Eds) (2008)
Passionate Leadership in Education
Sage

Buck, A (2012, 2nd edition)
What Makes a Great school?
United Learning

Buck, A, Tomlinson, O & Took, J (2014)
What Makes a Great Middle Leader?
United Learning

Cain, S (2012)
Quiet
Viking

Collins, J (2003)
Good to Great
Random House

Covey, S (2006)
The Speed of Trust
Simon & Schuster

De Pree, M (1992)
Leadership Jazz
Doublday

Denning, S (2007)
The Secret Language of Leadership
Jossey-Bass

Drucker, P.F (2009)
Managing in a Time of Great Change
Harvard Business Review Press

Einstein, A (1950)
Out of My Later Years
Thames & Hudson

Fullan, M (2008)
The Six Secrets of Change
Jossey-Bass

Fullan, M & Hargreaves, A (1992)
What's Worth Fighting for in Your School?'
OUP

Fullan, M (2001)
Leading in a Culture of Change
Jossey-Bass

Fullan, M (2004)
The Moral Imperative of School Leadership
Sage

Fullan, M (2014)
The Principal and Three Keys to Maximising Impact
Jossey-Bass

Goffee, R & Jones, G (2006)
Why Should Anybody be Led By You?
Harvard Business Review Press

Goleman, D (2002)
The New Leaders, Transforming the Art of School Leadership
Sphere

Goleman, D (2013)
Focus, The Hidden Driver of Excellence
Bloomsbury

Gardner, H (1995)
Leading Minds: Anatomoy of Leadership
Basic Books

Gawande, A (2008)
Better – A Surgeon's Notes on Performance
Profile Books

Handy, C.B (1990)
Inside Organisations
BBC Books

Handy, C.B (1997)
The Hungry Spirit
Hutchinson

Hargreaves, A & Shirley, D (2009)
The Fourth Way
Corwen

Hargreaves, D.H, & Finch, D (2006)
A New Shape for Schooling
SSAT

Hargreaves, D.H (2010)
Creating a Self-Improving School System
NCSL

Harris, A (2008)
Distributed School Leadership
Corwen

Hopkins, D (2001)
School Improvement for Real
Routledge Falmer

Jonsson, B (2001)
Ten Thoughts About Time
Constable

Kegan, R & Lahey, L..L (2003)
How The Way We Talk Can Change The Way We Lead
Jossey Bass

Kirtman, L (2013)
Leadership and Teams: The Missing Piece of the Education Reform Puzzle
Pearson Education

Krause, D (1997)
The Way of the Leader
Nicholas Brearley Publishing

Leithwood, K, Day, C, & Sammons, P Harris, A & Hopkins, D (2006)
Seven Strong Claims about Effective School Leadership
National College of School Leadership

Louis, K.S, & Miles, M.B (1990)
Improving the Urban High School
Teacher's College Press

McGilchrist, B, Myers, K & Reed, J (2004 2nd Edition)
The Intelligent School
Sage

Mandela, N (1994)
Long Walk to Freedom
Little Brown

Mowat, M, Corrigan, J & Long, D (2009)
The Success Zone
Global Publishing

Pendleton, D & Furnham, A (2013)
Leadership: All you need to know
Palgrave Macmillan

PriceWaterhouseCoopers (2007)
Independent Report into School Leadership
DfES Publications

Robinson, V (2011)
Student Centred Leadership
Jossey-Bass

Senge, P.M (2006)
The Fifth Discipline: The art and practice of the Learning Organisation
Doubleday

Sergiovanni, T (2001)
Leadership: What's in it for Schools?
Routledge

Smith, A (2011)
High Performers, The Secret of Successful Schools
Crown House

Sternberg, R.J.(2005)
International Journal of Leadership in Education
A Model of Educational Leadership

Stoll, L, Firth D & Earl, L (2003)
It's about Learning (and it's About Time)
Routledge Falmer

Syed, M (2010)
Bounce, The Myth of Talent and the Power of Practice
Fourth Estate

Van Maurik, J (2001)
Writers on Leadership
Penguin

West-Burnham, J & O'Sullivan, H (2011)
Leading and Managing Schools
Sage

West-Burnham, J & Harris, D (2015)
Leadership Dialogues –Conversations & Activities for Leadership Teams
Crown House Publishing

Whelan, F (2009)
Lessons Learned: How Good Policies Produce better schools
Fenton Whelan

Woods, D.C & Dowling, S (2014)
The A-Z of School Improvement through PE & Sport
United Learning

Woods, D.C & Brighouse, T.M (2015)
The Story of London Challenge
London Leadership Strategy

Woods, D.C & Macfarlane, R (Eds)
The Nine Pillars of Greatness
London Leadership Strategy

About London Leadership Strategy

The London Leadership Strategy (LLS) is a not-for-profit organisation run and led by serving headteachers and is born out of London Challenge, working to keep its spirit and mission alive. LLS is one of the largest providers of school-to-school support. It has an extensive network of National Leaders of Education (NLEs), Teaching Schools and schools providing support across the country. LLS's programmes support all schools at every point of their development journey - with programmes covering everything from school improvement to maintaining outstanding provision, pupil progress, leadership and peer-to-peer support.

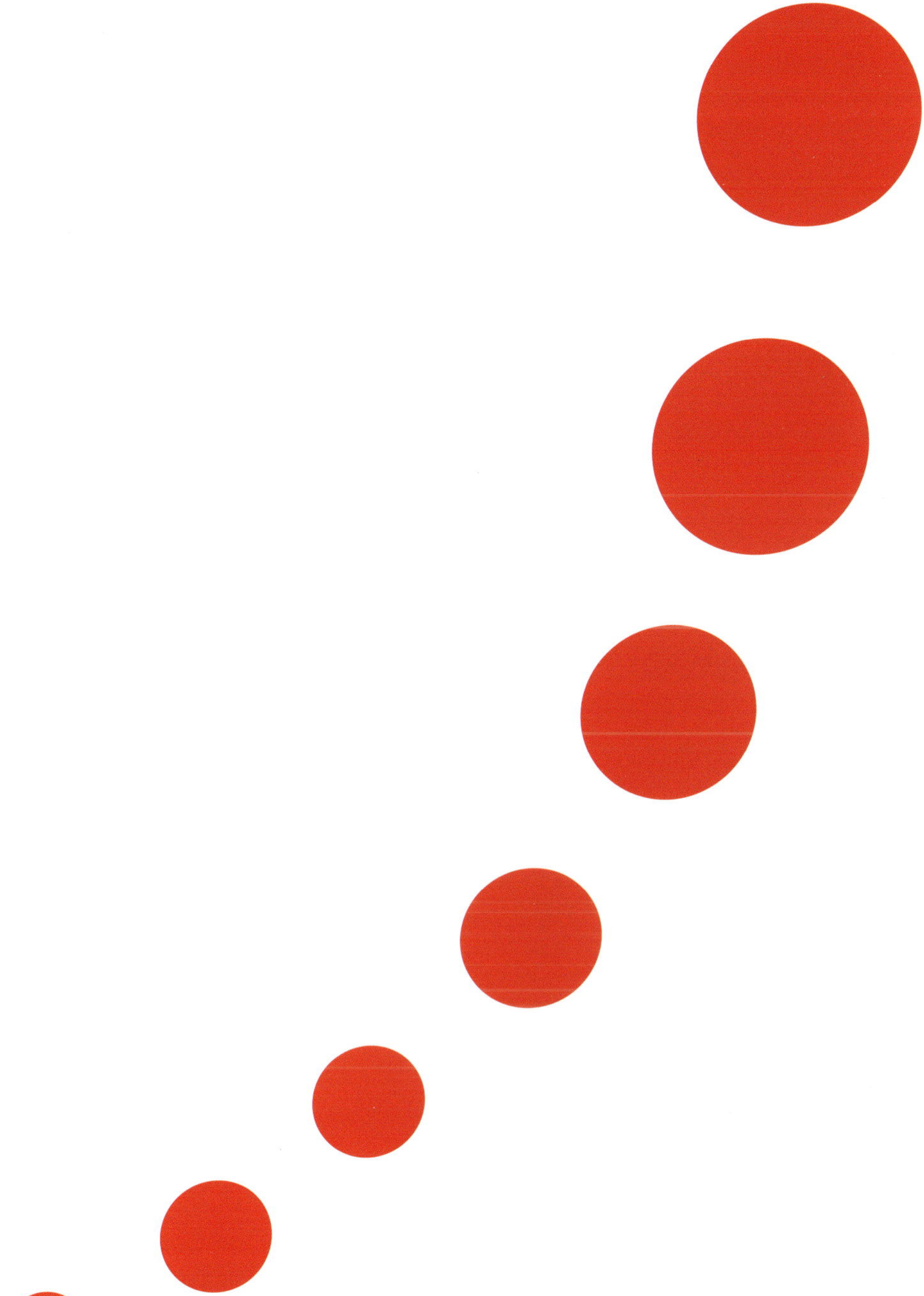